W9-AKA-396

JESUS GOES TO THE MARKETPLACE

A story of what might have happened one day when Jesus was a child.

CAROLYN MULLER WOLCOTT

Illustrated by Nell Fisher

JEFFERSONVILLE TOWNSHIP PUBLIC LIBRARY
JEFFERSONVILLE, INDIANA

ISBN 0-687-09005-9

 JUL -- 1999

COPYRIGHT © 1963, 1999 BY ABINGDON PRESS
ALL RIGHTS RESERVED.

ABINGDON PRESS
MANUFACTURED IN HONG KONG

99 00 01 02 03 04 05 06 07 08 – 10 9 8 7 6 5 4 3 2 1

#5139550

Skip, skip, skip along the dusty road.

Jesus smiled up at Mary, his mother.

He patted baby Joses on the hand.

He helped Joseph lead the little black goat.

For it was market day.

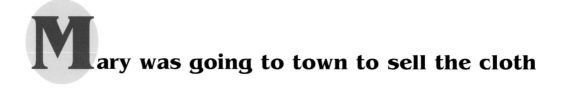

Mary was going to town to sell the cloth she had woven from wool, to buy barley and wheat for bread, to get peas and lentils for pottage, and to talk with the women in the marketplace.

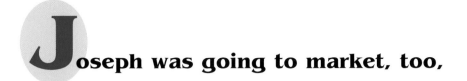

Joseph was going to market, too,

to sell the little black goat, to buy a

new saw for the carpenter shop, to find

sweet-smelling cedarwood to make a chest,

and to hear the latest news brought by

strangers from far away.

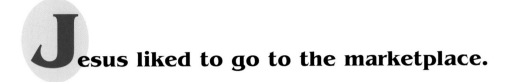

Jesus liked to go to the marketplace.

He liked to listen to tales told by storytellers.

He liked to hear of faraway lands from the camel

drivers. He liked to run in and out among

the crowds with his friends. And today he had

two coins in the purse in his belt.

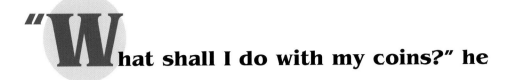

"**What shall I do with my coins?**" he

wondered. "**Shall I buy my mother some**

jewels to wear? Or a clay rattle for Joses?

Shall I buy a tool for the carpenter shop?

Or a pomegranate for me to eat?"

He skipped from booth to booth in the

marketplace. He stopped before the potter's

corner. He looked at the pots and bowls all

made of clay. He watched a woman who

bought a water jar.

Then he skipped on.

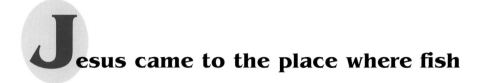esus came to the place where fish

were sold, fresh from the Sea of Galilee.

He listened to the fishermen talk of boats

and storms and mending nets. He looked at

the big fish and the small speckled ones.

"Someday I'll go to the sea," he said,

"and watch the men in their boats catching fish."

And he skipped on through the crowd in

the marketplace.

Jesus watched the farmers sell their grain. He saw a farmer dip his wooden measuring cup into the wheat. He saw the cup so full the wheat ran over. He watched the farmer pour grain into a skin bag.

"He is an honest farmer," thought Jesus.

"He gives the people who buy his grain more than they ask for."

And on he ran up the narrow street.

Jesus met a shepherd with a flock of

sheep. The shepherd was a rough man.

He had come from the desert. He had sheep

and bags of wool to trade for barley

and wheat.

Jesus patted a woolly lamb. "He

is like the lamb we have at home," he said.

And he hurried along.

He saw Ezra sitting in the corner of

the marketplace.

Ezra had a goose-quill pen stuck behind

his ear. He wrote messages for people who

could not write.

Ezra saw Jesus. "Any messages for

me to write?" he called.

"No, thank you," answered Jesus.

"Someday I'll be able to write."

And on through the market place he skipped.

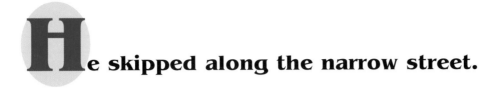

He skipped along the narrow street.

He ran 'round a corner and met Barsabbas.

Barsabbas was the basket man. Barsabbas

made baskets for the farmers' grain,

sandals for people's feet, mats for

the floors of houses, and ropes for tying up

donkeys and horses. Barsabbas made them

from rushes that grew by the stream.

"I hope you sell many baskets," called

Jesus as he skipped along the street.

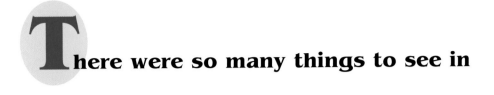

There were so many things to see in

the marketplace. There were so many

things two coins could buy.

Then Jesus saw Benjamin. Benjamin

sat by the wall of the town, all alone. He

could not see, so he could not work.

"He is hungry," thought Jesus.

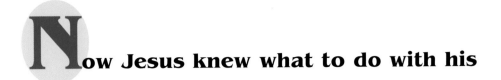ow Jesus knew what to do with his

two coins. He ran to Benjamin. He dropped

his coins into Benjamin's hand.

They jingled as they fell.

"They're for you, Benjamin," Jesus

called. "All for you."

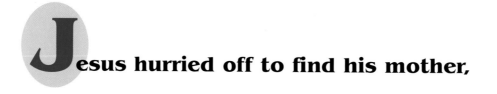

Jesus hurried off to find his mother,

Mary, and baby Joses and Joseph.

He wanted to tell them Benjamin was happy.

And Jesus was happy too.

3 1861 00389 2443

je W8492j

Wolcott, Carolyn Muller.

Jesus goes to the market
 place

**Jeffersonville Township Public
Library**
P.O. Box 1548
Jeffersonville, IN 47130